The Ultimate Guide To Buying A Car

How To Buy A Car Without Getting Ripped Off

George K.

Table of Contents

Introduction

Chapter 1: Do You Need a Car?

Chapter 2: Your Budget

Chapter 3: New or Used

Chapter 4: What Type of Car Do You Need?

Chapter 5: Internal and External Considerations

Chapter 6: How to Finance Your Purchase

Chapter 7: Insurance Options

Chapter 8: Common Pitfalls to Avoid

Conclusion

Introduction

I want to thank you and congratulate you for purchasing the book, *"The Ultimate Guide To Buying A Car: How to Buy A Car Without Getting Ripped Off"*.

This book contains proven steps and strategies on how to go about buying a car. Some authors argue that there is only 1 primary consideration, and that is actual need. They argue that price, brand new, insurance, etc., are all secondary considerations.

To some extent, this is true. But you also have to consider that an automobile is a mix between a need and a want. Hence, purists who argue otherwise really don't get how the automobile industry and man's fascination with the same, works. To be quite frank about it, if you think of an automobile as a purely need based consumer good, there is very little need for it in the city, as well as other areas were mass transportation is predominant.

This eBook can be summed up in a few words: Think about your purchase, step back, assess the situation, and make a reasonable but firm offer. In addition, the purchase price alone should not be your sole consideration for buying a car. There are also additional expenses that come with it i.e. petrol, insurance, maintenance, opportunity cost, etc.

So why should you listen to my advice? Aside from the fact that I have done research about techniques used car salesmen used, and I am also the happy owner of a couple of automobiles. One is a relatively new sedan (less than 2 years, bought brand new), and the other is a second hand pick up I've been using for several years now.

Thanks again for purchasing this book. I hope you enjoy it!

© **Copyright 2014 by George K. - All rights reserved.**

This document is geared towards providing exact and reliable information in regards to the topic and issue covered. The publication is sold with the idea that the publisher is not required to render accounting, officially permitted, or otherwise, qualified services. If advice is necessary, legal or professional, a practiced individual in the profession should be ordered.

- From a Declaration of Principles which was accepted and approved equally by a Committee of the American Bar Association and a Committee of Publishers and Associations.

In no way is it legal to reproduce, duplicate, or transmit any part of this document in either electronic means or in printed format. Recording of this publication is strictly prohibited and any storage of this document is not allowed unless with written permission from the publisher. All rights reserved.

The information provided herein is stated to be truthful and consistent, in that any liability, in terms of inattention or otherwise, by any usage or abuse of any policies, processes, or directions contained within is the solitary and utter responsibility of the recipient reader. Under no circumstances will any legal responsibility or blame be held against the publisher for any reparation, damages, or monetary loss due to the information herein, either directly or indirectly.

Respective authors own all copyrights not held by the publisher.

The information herein is offered for informational purposes solely, and is universal as so. The presentation of the information is without contract or any type of guarantee assurance.

The trademarks that are used are without any consent, and the publication of the trademark is without permission or backing by the trademark owner. All trademarks and brands within this book are for clarifying purposes only and are the owned by the owners themselves, not affiliated with this document.

Chapter 1: Do You Need a Car?

The need for a car transcends 100% pure utility. Yes, you can have a safe, comfortable, convenient means of public transport. But sometimes you want more. You want the freedom and luxury to dictate where you go and who you ride with.

Purely Utilitarian Perspective

Purists argue that there are 2 reasons a person would actually need a car. First, is because there is no other feasible means of transportation. Second, even if there is, owning your own car is cheaper, in the midterm and long term, even after factoring in purchase price, petrol, upkeep, and insurance, among others.

The Reasonable Perspective

The real question should be, will a car improve your quality of life? The answer to that depends on a lot of factors. Below are a few considerations:

- Will you be able to get to work more conveniently?

- Will you and/or your family be safer?

- Will owning a car open new doors for personal growth i.e. job, relationship, hobbies, etc.

- Will travel be faster?

The 20% Rule

Considering your regular income and expenditures, can you really afford a car, the petrol, the added maintenance, and insurance? If you are purchasing a car outright, how much of your savings will it deplete? As a general rule, you want the car you purchase to leave you with 20% savings. If you are taking an auto loan, how much of your regular income will it use up? As a general rule, you don't want your monthly amortizations to go higher than 20%.

The reason for this is because a car is a huge purchase. If you can't afford to make one, then don't. The truth is, the only reason one should buy an automobile on the negative, is because it is necessary for transportation. Meaning, there is no feasible alternative means of going from one point to another. Of course, when you absolutely want to, you should at least make sure that the benefits outweighs the cost – not just of buying the car but of keeping it – by far.

Chapter 2: Your Budget

How much should you spend to purchase a car? The answer depends on your needs, lifestyle and actual financial status. Below are a few considerations.

Income and Expense Worksheet

How much do you make and spend in a month? Knowing the answer to this question determines in large part your budget ro lack of it, for the purchase of an automobile. It's simple. Who will pay for the car? If the answer is you alone, then you only make an income and expense worksheet for yourself. If there are others who will share the expense with you, then you can add their total and monthly contributions. It might also be a good idea to make them do an income and expense worksheet. Just to make sure they actually have the capacity to make the contribution.

List down all your sources of income and how much you actually make on a regular basis i.e. monthly. Overtime pay that is not part of your regular income is not included. Deduct the taxes that you pay on your income. Now you have your NET income.

List down all the expenses you make in a month. Start with necessary expenses like utilities, groceries, education, taxes i.e. property taxes, home mortgage, personal insurance, phone, internet, etc. Move on to luxury expenditures like your premium cable subscription.

Unaccountable

Make sure to know exactly how much money you spend each month. Chances are your expense worksheet says one thing and your actual money on hand shows another. The difference should be resolved via miscellaneous expenditures. In other words, anything that you can't track, add it to miscellaneous expense.

10% Savings Account

It is also a good idea to minus 10% off your net income and place it in a savings account. This way you have money saved up for a rainy day! This should not form part of your budget for buying a car!

How Much is Left?

Do you still have money left over to buy a car? Be honest here. If you have a modest savings account, remember the 20% rule. Now, if you use that as down payment, will your surplus income be enough to pay for a car that meets your needs?

Chapter 3: New or Used

The question of buying used or brand new is both simple and tricky. It is simple because there is a specific breed of individuals who can own used cars. For everyone else, it's better to buy new cars. All you need to do is go over a check list. The hard part is finding the perfect used automobile for you.

A brand new car on the other hand is a lot more expensive. It is expensive, not because it is so much better than used cars. It is expensive because it hasn't depreciated in value yet. For those of you not in the know, a brand new car depreciates in value, the very moment you take it out for the first drive. On average, an automobile depreciates in value 10% to 20% per year.

Used Car Owner Checklist

There are 2 types of potential used car owners. First there are those who buy cars that are slightly used, probably several months to a couple of years. These cars are also still being produced by their manufacturers. Hence, it is as if you bought brand new. In which case, you would either need a trusted mechanic or be a passable mechanic yourself. You need to check: what's under the hood; what's under the chassis; what's under the upholstery, etc. You need to perform an extensive test drive. Simply put, you make sure that the automobile is not a lemon.

The second type of used car owner is one who is an expert mechanic and all around automobile enthusiast. These guys can look at an automobile, tell you what's wrong, and fix it! More importantly, they know the right people. As such, finding parts won't cost them an arm and a leg. Simply put, they can buy less than pristine condition used cars, fix it with relative ease, and still get a bargain.

Finding the Perfect Used Car

Where do you find the best used cars? Frankly speaking, it is better to look at classified ads and go straight to the owner. This way you have a better chance at driving down the asking price. This is as opposed to going to a used car dealership, where you've got several brokers who already have a piece of the action, hence a higher sticker price.

Remember, if you are not an expert mechanic, then bring one that you trust. Bring with you a check book so you look like you mean business. Now check everything! Ask for change oil receipts, repair history, look at the mileage meter, etc.

Making an Offer

If you are buying used cars, the price is negotiable. This is especially true if you are buying from the actual owner. Ask for a quote, and then make your counter offer. Remember, your initial offer must be lower than your maximum bid. This allows you to haggle with the seller.

Who should make the initial offer? It is best to let the seller give you a figure. Now counter that figure with an amount that is lower than your maximum bid. The general rule is for your initial bid to be calculated so, if the seller and you meet halfway between his asking price and your initial offer, then the resulting amount is your maximum bid. For example, you have a maximum bid of $7,500. If the seller says $10,000; you say $5,000. This way, if you both haggle with the price, the midway point is $7,500.

What if the seller insists you make the first offer? In that case, subtract 30% off your maximum bid price. That should give you room to maneuver.

If you have misgivings with the car, ask for a quote and make a low ball offer. Ask to think it over for a couple of days. Remember, walking away, and sleeping it off, might just clear your head.

And for crying out loud, don't appraise the car, and keep muttering that it's perfect for you! Always say something nice about the car and then notice a defect. This shows the owner you appreciate the car but are hesitant. This allows you to drive the price lower. For example: I can't find anything wrong with the engine! You sure know how to take care of it! I only wished it had a different paint job, or a better set of wheels. Yup, I'll definitely have to change the wheels on this one.

Buying Brand New

If you have absolutely zero knowledge of how a car works, other than to drive the same, then it would be better for you to buy brand new. Otherwise, you would also need to have a very trusted mechanic by your side, and on call.

When buying brand new, the ideal is to pay in full. This will allow you to drive down the price of the automobile, 10% to 25% from its sticker/installment price. If you don't have that kind of cash, then you should at least have a 20% to 30% down payment. Then negotiate for a fix rate amortization that is payable as soon as possible. This should drive down the interest payments you make. Ask the dealer to remove all add-ons and accessories. You want a quote for the car alone and necessaries. If the seller insists on accessories, tell him to make a separate quote. But you also want a barebones quote for you to take home the car. If he says it's impossible, walk away. There are plenty of dealers out there!

Chapter 4: What Type of Car Do You Need?

The wrong way to go about this is to have a car in mind, and then try to rationalize its purchase by saying to yourself, 'this is the one I need'.

The right way to buy a car is to list down specific requirements. And then look for a car that fits the same. You can be as specific as you want. But you should try to categorize your lists by placing actual needs on side and preferences on the other. For example:

Needs:

- All in price does not exceed $10,000
- Seats 5 adults comfortably
- Airbags for the driver, passenger and sides
- Disc brakes with ABS

- Gasoline powered with average fuel economy

- A huge trunk that can fit your luggage and a medium sized dog crate

- No paint bubbles (indicating rust)

Preferences:
- Paddle shift

- Seat warmer/heater

- 16 inch wheels

- Genuine leather interior

- Red color

- Parking assist cameras

- GPS navigation

- Superb sound system

Is the Car Manufacturer?

Yes, the brand name is important. You need to make sure that you are buying from a manufacturer that is known to churn out automobiles that stand the test of time. It does not necessarily need to be a European brand mind you. Select your top 3 brands. Make sure to prioritize road safety test results, as well as resale value based on actual deterioration. This is because, in most cases, the cars with the best resale value are those that stand the test of time. Cases in point are the Toyota land cruiser or the BMW E46, Fourth generation, 1998-2006.

Car Make

Do you need a sports car, sedan, minivan, a pickup truck, or any other car make? Take for example SUV's that tend to be more expensive than a sedan or a pickup. Do you really need to shell out an additional $3,000 for an SUV when you have never in your life gone out of the city? Or is a low mileage sedan a better fit for you? Granted, you decide which car to buy, but if you are on a tight budget, then you need to start prioritizing.

Should you be eyeing that sports car when you have a baby on the way? A sedan won't work for an everyday workhorse, in which case a pickup truck or van might be a better choice.

Car Model

The model of the car is also important. You need to realize that even the best car manufacturers have been known to turn a lemon or two. Take for example, Volvo. These guys are known for quality automobiles. So why are their SUV crossovers so damn temperamental?! Even Mercedes isn't immune to lemon cars. Take for example the dreaded M class; it doesn't look great, it doesn't work great, but it's still expensive as hell!

Chapter 5: Internal and External Considerations

When buying a car, you need to know the materials used, from the steel body, chassis, engine, electronic components, upholstery, safety gear, etc. You are looking for a car that is durable, cost efficient, safe, and comfortable.

The Body

Majority of buyers see the design of the body and its general aesthetics. Of course you want a car that is pleasing to your eyes. You want something that fits your preferences. But you also want steel that is thicker than a tin can! Perform a walk around of the car. Push on the steel panels at appropriate areas i.e. door panel, hood, roof, etc. Give it a few gentle knocks. You don't want a car with a steel body that gives in when you exert the slightest force. You don't want panels that sound hollow and thin.

How's the Paint Job?

The best paint jobs don't only look good; it also offers protection for your car exterior. If you know someone who has the same make and model, pay him a visit. Ask to look at the car. Pay special attention to the places where steel panels have been welded together. You don't want to see rust marks and bubbling on the paint. To be clear, a certain degree of rust is acceptable for older models that have been exposed to the elements. But rust erosions are an absolute no-no.

The Interior

You want an interior that is roomy, comfy, and well made. In this generation, unless you are buying premium brands or top of the line models, you will inevitably see plastic or imitation leather. Just make sure it's thick, joined together, and ergonomic enough.

Pay special attention to leg room and head clearance. You should also sit in the driver's side and go over general visibility. Open up the lights on the dashboard. Test drive it. Perform a few turns. Look at the pillars that support the windshield and roof. Is it overly obstructive of your view?

Safety Features

Nowadays, multiple airbags, disc brakes, ABS, and side beam bars come standard in most cars. Prioritize the same, instead of ogling the 10 inch LED display, or the Dolby surround system.

Under the Hood

You want an engine that has enough power for your personal and expected needs. For example, a minivan does not need to have a big block v8. You don't need the 4wd function if you aren't an outdoorsman. What you do need is fuel economy and durability. A quiet ride is also a good idea. A few extra horsepower should also be considered.

Ride Comfort

This refers both to the driver and passengers. How's the suspension. How's the air conditioning and heater? Is the car nimble on the steering wheel or is it sluggish and unresponsive? How's the transmission, clutch and gear shift?

Chapter 6: How to Finance Your Purchase

Majority of purchasers, especially in the brand new category do not pay in full. Rather, they finance their purchase via an auto loan. Below are a few tips you should remember when applying for an auto loan.

When to Apply?

Should you apply before or after you walk into a car dealership? Majority of the time you want to see visit your local car dealer first. This will allow you to get a feel for how much you actually need to pay in terms of down payment, installment, petrol, insurance, maintenance, etc.

1. Talk to the dealer and get written quotes.

2. Go over your financial records. Remember your income and expense worksheet.

3. Pull out your credit reports and purchase 1 credit score. It's best to pullout your 3 reports from the top 3 credit unions. Be prepared to see different reports. However the variation should not be more than 10%.

4. Asses your situation. If you have enough down payment, enough surplus income and an excellent credit score, then go ahead and apply for a car loan.

5. Some dealers like to have you file the application in house, but it is a better idea to have a couple of options. Compare in house financing with bank/lender financed car loans.

6. READ THE FINE PRINT! Make sure you understand what happens if you

default. Make sure the interest rate is fixed. Make sure that you have flexibility when it comes to place of payment. Make sure you get adequate notice before you are called in for default. What is your grace period?

7. Scrutinize the closing costs. Make sure you are not being made to pay more and for things that are unrelated to the purchase.

Timing is Key

The worst time to buy a car is when there is a buyer's market. This is especially true when a new model has just been released. If you can, wait several months to see how the car actually performs and read reviews regarding the same. This is also ample time for the manufacturer to introduce upgrades.

The best time to buy is just before a model is changed. This means you are buying a car with full upgrades and at its cheapest. Simply put, car manufacturers have to dispose of the old stock to give way to the new. Of course, the trade off is, after several months, a new model replaces yours.

If you insist on buying the newest model, then time your purchase when a dealer is hurrying to meet a quota. This is usually before the end of each quarter and semester. At this time, car dealers and the sales person is more susceptible to negotiate. He doesn't need to make much for the sale. All he needs is to make and exceed the quota to get a bonus.

Go to Several Dealers

In relation to an agents quota, they have this unwritten rule that only 1 agent per branch handles the same customer. That is why it is a good idea to visit 3 to 5 dealers. This way you get a better chance of talking to an agent who is looking to hit his quota. There is also the fact that, every time you talk to an agent, you become better at haggling for a better deal. When all else fails, show them a quote from another dealer. Now ask them to top that offer!

When in Doubt

Go back to your income and expense worksheet. Remember, auto dealers, banks, lenders, etc., have a tendency to try and sell you an auto loan amortization you can't really afford. Yes, it is within your income, but considering your expenses, you really can't afford it.

Compute for Total Loan Amount

How much exactly will you pay in total, if you pay interest and principal for the entire loan duration? Some consumers don't do this, or do this too late. As a result they get shocked at the amount they actually pay for interest payments.

Important Reminders

If you have below excellent credit ratings, it would be best to wait a couple of months and fix your credit report. This can be done by paying your debts due and demandable. This will work for your benefit because there is a significant difference between the interest rate given to individuals with bad credit vis a vis excellent credit rating.

If you have below excellent credit, and you need the car ASAP, then you need to increase your down payment to say 30% to 50%.

Try to pay the loan as soon as possible. Remember, each installment means another interest payment. Therefore you want a loan that you can pay and has the lowest number of installment payments.

Chapter 7: Insurance Options

Most brand new units come with standard comprehensive insurance, for 1 to 2 years. After that, it's up to you to find an insurer. The author suggests, that you keep your options open. Try to bargain for a quote that includes and excludes insurance. Take note of the insurance coverage.

Second hand units NEED to have up to date insurance. This way you know how much you will be paying and even continue the insurance, albeit in a different name. Now verify with the named insurance company on the status of the same and claims made on the car.

What is the Minimum Requirement?

The answer depends on where you live. Mandatory minimum requirements usually include collisions that cause damage to property and injury to person/ up to a specific amount per claimant. In addition, there is also a total payable amount for all claims for a single collision.

For example: the max payable amount per claimant is $1,000. The max payable amount for a single collision is $4,800. So if there are 6 claimants, and each of them is entitled to $1,200 each, then your insurance covers only $800 per person. The money not covered by insurance will usually be paid out of your pocket.

Is Comprehensive Insurance Worth It?

The answer depends. First you need to understand that comprehensive insurance usually involves the following:

- Collision causing damage to property and injury to persons
- Theft
- vandalism
- Fire
- Flood
- Falling objects

As a general rule, yes comprehensive insurance is worth it. For one, you need the insurance in order to comply with the law. Also, you can't renew your car's license without adequate insurance. Just makes sure you have the minimum covered, and don't pay for risks that are out of this world.

Tip: If you are not a frequent traveler, opt to remove travel insurance form your coverage, if any. When you do travel, you can purchase temporary travel insurance that cover specific dates.

Find a Third Party Insurer

The biggest advantage to finding your own insurer, is you can pretty much dictate personalize your insurance. You can also provide specific information that can lower your car insurance rate. For example, you can remove risks that you will not need i.e. fire insurance, theft insurance, etc. Provided of course you still meet the minimum requirements set by your state. You can then include risks that you know your automobile will be subjected to i.e. snow related damage, travel insurance, destructive cyclone, etc.

For example, if you live and stay in a relatively dry place, with very little chance of flooding, you might want to haggle for the removal of flood insurance and the addition of travel insurance, for long distance out of state travel, which you often do.

Driving History

Your driving history is a factor when taking out insurance. Therefore, if this is a couple's car, and ownership really is not an issue, it would be best to name as owner, the one with the cleanest driving history i.e. no DUI, no prior accidents, no excessive tickets, etc.

I Own a Garage!

If you own an indoor garage, and usually park your automobile via secure parking at work, then it is best to allege the same. This is because this would minimize the risk of theft. It doesn't mean you fully drop, theft as a risk, but it means the insurer has to lower the risk of theft.

Make and Model

Some insurers will insist on higher insurance rates for specific makes and model. For example, a sports car has higher premium payments than a minivan. An older used car has higher insurance rates while newer cars have lower rates. The average difference is around $50 to $200 per premium payment, depending on the make and model. Another example, insurers know what makes and model are reliable. A Toyota Camry has lower insurance rates than a Mitsubishi Gallant. That should tell you that insurers are less worried about the former breaking down, than the latter. For some reason, Nissan has very high insurance rates, as opposed to Honda. Again, that should tell you a great deal about reliability.

Chapter 8: Common Pitfalls to Avoid

A car is not rocket science. You don't need a degree to buy your perfect car. However, you need to have a certain degree of common sense and control. This way you actually buy the car that you need, not the one the dealer tells you, you need.

Going Over Budget

You know how much money you make. You know how much you have left after deducting expenses. You know how much savings you have. You want the dealer to work for you. You don't want to work for the dealer. So tell him what you need, what you can afford, and let him give you his best offer. If he does not have what you need, move on to the next dealer.

Manage Your Expectations

If you are buying second hand, don't expect to smell that new car smell. Don't expect to have a pristine interior. Don't expect to have a perfect coat of paint. And by the way, as a general rule, a well maintained car loses 1 to 2 horsepower a year. Most cars lose around 3 to 5 horses, annually. The trick is knowing a well maintained car and determining if it is a good deal.

Don't Buy Online

This is just stupid. You do not buy a car without looking at it, scrutinizing it, driving it, etc. when your seller tells you that it is "was is where is", then you better have your guard up, and a very good mechanic to scrutinize every inch of that automobile. Don't just inspect it inside a garage with poor lighting. Bring it over to an auto shop. Have the car raised so you can see what's under the chassis! Remove a few side panels to see the condition of the steel inside. The last thing you want is to buy a restored outside but flooded inside car. When we say flooded, we mean, it got swallowed up by flood waters!

When in Doubt, Sleep on It

If you cannot find the car that meets all your requirements, but you have a very good contender, what do you do? You don't go into a haggling war with the seller. First, make sure that whatever requirement is not met is negligible. Second, you low ball the seller. When the seller says no, ask him to give you a couple of days.

If the seller takes the bait on your low ball offer, good for you. If the seller says no, then you have more time to get your mind straight. Remember, walking away allows you to think carefully, as opposed to making an impulsive purchase.

Smoke Emission

Make sure that a second hand unit can pass smoke emissions test. Otherwise, you might end up with a car without a license plate.

Don't Name Your Son as Owner

If you are buying a car for your child, then you want to be the registered owner. Sure, putting the car under his name is a good gesture and all. But it will also increase the insurance premiums! Remember, teenagers as well as individuals in their early 20's have the highest insurance rates.

Don't Pay for Useless Premium Accessories

Nowadays it's easy to buy authentic accessories for a cheaper price. On the other hand, car dealers like to overprice these said items. Do you really need a floor mat that costs you 5 times what you can buy outside? Do you really need a rear spoiler that can cost you a thousand dollars? Do you really need to have wood grain panels on your car? By the way, built-in GPS can sometimes be inferior to an independently bought unit.

But you do need ABS. You do need disc brakes. You do need air conditioning and heating. If you are buying secondhand, you want a good pair of tires. As much as possible you want as a close to stock as possible. That is, unless modified cars are your thing. If it is modified, you want to know who did the modification. You don't want a run of the mill patch job. You want someone who knows what he was doing.

Pay Attention to the Engine and Transmission!

Majority of buyers get awed by the creature comforts of a car. They fail to properly research the engine, transmission, and its track record. You want an engine and transmission that is reliable, durable, and has enough horsepower for your needs. If you are buying diesel powered then a certain degree of noise is acceptable. But too much noise can get irritating. So be aware of the same!

Get Owner Feedback

You've got a relative, friend, or even a neighbor who has the same car you want to buy. You don't bother to get feedback from the same. You buy the car anyway. You visit a family get together and your brother tells you, you should have asked him first. The car both of you bought is a lemon. You and your neighbor meet at the gas station or grocery, using the same car. Now your neighbor tells you to be wary of the transmission, it get's sticky after 1 year.

Read Online Reviews

Go online and look at crash test statistics. Read owner feedback. Don't just believe the dealer when he/she tells you that all is well! Take note of all the recalls happening left and right! Would you want to be subjected to that?

Recall No-no's

If a specific make and model has been recalled more than once for component defects, then scratch the same from your want list. One recall can be excusable, unless it is a very important component like, part of the engine. Take for example the massive recall of Isuzu Trooper. During its heyday, the trooper was a Mitsubishi Pajero and Toyota Land Cruiser competitor. It had power, durability, and unlike the competition, a very plush interior! But, Isuzu started recalling Troopers for engine defect. It came to a point, where it got so bad, the entire Trooper line was discontinued.

Repaint Woes

If the car you bought has been repainted, then you need to know by whom. This is because you never know why the repaint was actually done. It could have been because the owner did not like the original color. It could be because it had so many bumps that it had to be repainted. Bear in mind that a poorly done paint job can result in exterior woes later on. Some paint jobs bubble up due to poor application of paint. Other paint jobs stripped the car odd its original paint, but did not perform proper rust proofing. Patch work paint jobs discolor aftertime, and you've got a visibly different coat of paint on one part of your car. Bear in mind that majority of the time, a car with pristine stock paint has a higher resale value than repainted cars. That is the repaint job was superb!

Car Crash Woes

Make sure to check if you are buying a car that has been subjected to a collision. This usually means a repair job, a paint, job, and several other modifications made. In some cases the crash might have even compromised the structural integrity of the car. Engine problems may also pop up If the collision somehow hit the engine and transmission compartment. The chassis might also have a problem. If you can, avoid a car that has history of collision. Remember, collision/accident disclosure by the seller is a must. If a car is less than 5 years old, an owner is duty bound to put in writing 25% or more damage due to accident/collision, etc. Even brand new cars may be subject to damage. The dealer has to tell you any damage exceeding 5%. None disclosure is criminal in nature!

Cheap Replacement Parts

If you are buying second hand, make sure to check for replacement parts. As much as possible you want the car to be stock. But if there are replacement then you want the same to be original or of superior character. Take for example, headlight sockets. Most owners change cheap plastic sockets with more expensive porcelain ones. That's okay, provided the replacement is done properly and the parts are of good quality.

Worst case scenario, is the engine was replaced. If that is the case, make sure the proper modification has been made to the license and registration of the car. Otherwise, you might not be able to renew the registration.

Don't just look at the engine, even windows, door panels, dashboard etc., can be replaced. Make sure you've got original parts! Not cheap knock offs!

Warranty/Guarantee in Writing

Brand new cars have pretty standard warranty and guarantee contracts. Just make sure that you have an authorized service center near you. Second hand cars are a bit more troublesome. First, you want to get the repair information and service information to aid you with the repair shop. Verify with the authorized repair shop or mechanic on the servicing and repairs conducted, before closing the deal. This is because some sellers try to hide repair jobs and just give you incomplete servicing information. When you verify with the shop you suddenly realize that there have been dozen of jobs done to the car!

Worst, if the owner did not go to authorized repair centers and did the repairs on his own or via third party repairers. Good luck tracking the information down. The best you can do is perform a thorough inspection. If the repair information given to you does not match what you see, and repairs were not made in an authorized repair center, then walk away.

Insurance Woes

You want a car that is up to date on its insurance. First, if the insurance is not up to date, then you might end up paying penalties. Even if the same is waived, sporadically insured automobiles have higher insurance premiums. Why is that? Because insurers and buyers can't track what has actually happened to the car.

One way to verify if the seller is up front with you regarding the damage done to the car, or the number of times it has been repaired is via insurance claims. If you have complete insurance then you can pretty much track every insurance claim made. Seldom will you see an owner who will not try to claim on insurance for any damage done. If the damage and repair information given to you does not balance out with records from the insurance agency, then you know you've got a shady seller.

Conclusion

Thank you again for purchasing this book!

I hope this book was able to help you to make an informed car purchase.

The next step is to actually apply the information, tips, techniques you've read. Don't be that guy who reads an eBook, but doesn't apply what he's learned. Remember, faith in humanity is okay. But when you are buying a car, you want everything to be up front, in writing, and verifiable.

Finally, if you enjoyed this book, then I'd like to ask you for a favor, would you be kind enough to leave a review for this book on Amazon? It'd be greatly appreciated!

Thank you and good luck!

Printed in Great Britain
by Amazon